The Power of Uncertainty

by

Hoyt Hilsman and Dennis Palumbo

The Power of Uncertainty

"The only thing that makes life possible is a permanent, intolerable uncertainty: not knowing what comes next."
Ursula LeGuin

"Plainly speaking, there's no such thing as certainty; there are only people who are certain."
Charles Renouvier

Once in a while, Stacey has to work late. She takes the last train home and walks the few blocks to her condo. On this particular night, the streets are deserted and she has a sense of growing dread. The streetlights are out and it's a moonless night. She squints down the street, searching for shadows amongst the trees, quickening her pace as she draws her coat tightly around her.

Her senses are heightened as she listens for strange sounds, and even the rustling of the leaves pumps up her anxiety. Her rational mind tells her over and over that there's nothing to be afraid of. But her heart is racing and the adrenaline is beginning to surge through her body. After what seems like an eternity, she arrives at her door. Her hands shaking, she fumbles with her keys. When she finally makes it inside her house, she is still trembling.

What is it that so frightened Stacey? No one threatened her. In fact, she had no reason to expect danger on this tranquil nighttime street. But in Stacey's situation, most of us would feel exactly the same, at least to some degree. Why?

Because, in the face of the unknown, or the unseen--in other words, the uncertain--

our primitive brains take over. *At the most basic level, we are wired for*

uncertainty.

In fact, the wiring is pretty simple. It's the "fight or flight" response. When

the hapless caveman--as often envisioned in a wry *New Yorker* cartoon--encounters

a saber-toothed tiger, his choice is clear. Either put up a fight, or run like hell.

But what about all the *unseen* tigers? The shadowy unknown lurking down

a dark street? Or the insistent fear of flying on an airplane during a terrorist threat

alert? Or the anxiety of a new and uncertain career? Or even that of walking

down the aisle into the uncertainty of marriage?

Whatever uncertainty you're facing--whatever dark street you walk down,

whether real or metaphorical--your brain reacts pretty much the same way. In

simplest terms, the brain switches very quickly from normal physiological activity

to a state of high readiness. Upon encountering a threat, a tiny region at the base of

the brain sets off a system of neural and hormonal signals that prompt the adrenal

glands to release a surge of adrenaline and cortisol. Adrenaline elevates blood

pressure, increases heart rate, and boosts energy supply. Cortisone increases

glucose (sugars) in the bloodstream and multiplies the availability of substances

that repair tissues. This complex process also activates regions of the brain that

control mood, motivation and fear.

No matter what the threat, our brains will have the same response. However, there is one big difference between walking down a dark street and facing an uncertain career change, a difficult marriage or challenging economic times. Once Stacey makes it inside the door of her house, her heartbeat returns to normal, her blood pressure drops and the surge of adrenaline subsides. But when you are facing another kind of uncertainty--the kind that is ongoing and more abstract--your heartbeat may be *consistently* elevated, along with your blood pressure and adrenal output. Because most of the threats we face these days are not of the saber-toothed tiger variety, or even the shadowy street variety, our modern version of uncertainty tends to be more abstract, stress-related and prolonged.

The Era of Uncertainty

The fact is, we have more uncertainty in our contemporary world than a caveman ever dreamed possible, and considerably more than even our parents or grandparents experienced. We live in a fast-paced, rapidly changing world, where new technology and a flood of information cram our brains--and our limbic systems. As Nicholas Carr points out in *The Shallows*, similar to what Alvin Toffler before him pointed out in *Future Shock*, the pace of technological change is outdistancing our ability to process it, to understand it, to feel mastery over it. On a psychological, social and intellectual level, the speed of change can be overwhelming. Our poor brains can't keep up.

Take the economy, for instance. In generations past, people often had a job-- or at least a career--for life. Even if you weren't a highly-paid executive with a venerable company, assured of a pension and benefits, it was still a world with less uncertainty; a world where a decent job in a factory or delivering milk could pay a mortgage and feed a family. But those days are gone.

Today, in the midst of the Great Recession and the mortgage meltdown, when iconic corporations collapse and jobs are out-sourced; at a time that sees gender and social roles in flux, and battle lines being drawn in the Cultural Wars; in a new viral age that's created a twenty-four hour news and information cycle, we feel more uncertainty in our lives than ever before.   Our lives are full of stress. Governed, to a large extent, by a fear of the unknown.

The result is that many of us are running on the fight-or-flight reaction for a much longer period than nature intended. What may have been a good short-term response to threats on the ancient savannah has become a potentially harmful one in our post-modern lives. Why? Because research has shown that the effects of the response are cumulative. The chemical imbalances set in motion by the rush of noradrenalin are not reset to zero, but "stored" in the body, thus creating an elevated awareness of threat and sense of fear. A long-running, almost continuous activation of the fight-or-flight response--with its overexposure to cortisol and other hormones--can play havoc with your body's natural regulatory processes, leading to a greater risk of obesity, insomnia, heart disease, depression and physical illness.

Walls in Our Minds

We all respond to uncertainty with fear. It's built into our wiring, and literally impossible to avoid. People who plunge into uncertain, dangerous situations without an ounce of fear are clearly deluded and possibly clinically ill. Whether it's skydiving or mountain climbing, a hefty dose of fear is crucial to survival. But in less clear-cut cases of uncertainty--such as the specter of job loss or the threat of divorce, or even the everyday dilemmas of modern life--fear is a constant partner of uncertainty, as it should be. But fear of what? The potential for shame, for example, following a perceived "failure." Or, perhaps, the pain of rejection, whether personal or professional. Then there's the fear of illness, or that of reliving a traumatic event--both rooted in uncertainty--that can also trigger stinging feelings of dread.

It *is* true that different people respond to fear and uncertainty in different ways. Some people are simply more vulnerable to stress than others, due to the influence of those two well-known determinants, "nature and nurture." Like it or not, we human beings are the sum total of everything we inherently (that is, genetically) are, and everything we've experienced. If we've suffered emotional trauma, were exposed to unhealthy early-childhood family dynamics in dealing with change, have persistent low self-esteem, or struggle with physical or economic hardships, we're more likely to regard uncertainty as threatening. But no matter where uncertainty registers on our fear meter, it's a major part of the equation.

One more important point to note about our internal wiring for uncertainty: *a constantly heightened state of anxiety can seriously cloud our thinking.* How many times have we had the urge to act impulsively just to banish the fear and anxiety of a situation? As Stacey walks down the dark street, her mind is racing. She fights the urge to break into a run, even though she might easily risk falling and hurting herself. Or she considers crying for help, even though there is no one around to hear her. Part of our response to uncertainty is to try to make it disappear, to impulsively grasp for some sense of certainty--*anything* to calm the painful anxiety of the unknown.

Our ancient ancestors built primitive walls to seek shelter from the unknown--though real and ongoing--terrors of the outside world. However, those literal walls that we once built against a fierce and hostile world have now morphed into metaphorical walls, erected in our minds to protect us from the threatening uncertainty of our lives. These metaphorical walls--*our psychological defense mechanisms*--are powerful bulwarks against fear and the unknown, defending against the crashing waves of anxiety that can swamp our fragile sense of ourselves.

While there's a slightly pejorative connotation to the phrase "defense mechanism," implying weakness or inadequacy on the part of the person employing them, there's no doubt we all utilize such psychological defenses in our daily lives to some extent. They're an aspect of our emotional arsenal, as important--and irrefutable-- a part of our psyche as empathy, dread, awe, and capacity for joy. Sometimes conscious, sometimes not, psychological defense mechanisms are our primary weapon against the distress of uncertainty.

And there are as many variations in the design and construction of these psychological "walls" as there are people. Throughout history, thinkers have marveled at the myriad ways that people respond to stress--the coping skills and symptoms that people develop and exhibit. It's one of the most fascinating aspects of the human condition, but also one of the most mysterious. However, since the advent of the scientific age, there has been an accelerated, almost Herculean attempt to define and understand our psychological defense mechanisms. While there are abundant (and conflicting) theories about the origin and operation of psychological defense mechanisms, there's no dispute that humans employ a variety of mental tactics--consciously or not--in the struggle against the anxiety of the unknown. It's also clear that while our defense mechanisms provide a useful bulwark against fear and anxiety, they also can distort our perspective on reality, obstructing our growth and diluting our understanding of the world we live in.

The Quest for Certainty

Anthony has been working in the real estate industry for eleven years, making a good living. He's survived through the ups-and-downs of the market, and worked his way up to branch manager. But, since the housing crisis and the Great Recession, he's been clinging to his job like a life raft. The reality is that his job--and his future--may be in jeopardy. What is his strategy? Denial. Do a good job and hope for the best. Forget about sending out resumes or plotting a career change. If he doesn't worry about it, it won't happen. Not a very good strategy, but a classic defense mechanism.

Frieda is a religious person, stuck in a rocky marriage. She suspects her husband has been cheating on her, but she's afraid to confront him. She confides in her friends, who counsel her to leave the marriage, or at least seek help from a trained professional. She's talked to her pastor, but he isn't much help. So rather than take action, Frieda seeks solace in prayer. Of course, prayer can be a great aid in healing, and, once in a while, miracles actually happen. But as a strategy for facing reality, prayer is simply another defense mechanism--a quest for a certainty that does not exist.

In traditional psychological theory, defense mechanisms provide an indispensable service--they are our psychological armor against the unknown. And the field of psychology is filled with the classification and categorization of these mechanisms, from fantasy, self-delusion, and ritualistic thinking to a host of other defenses. But when you step back and look at the way these psychological "walls" operate, you see that they all serve the same purpose--to guard against the fear of the unknown.

What our psychological defenses give us is some sense of certainty, the belief that if we simply wish away uncertainty through faith, or obsessive planning, or fantasy, or any other of a host of "magical thoughts," then we will find the certainty we seek. Whether it's "the power of positive thinking" or the "Ten Keys to Happiness" or the proverbial "leap of faith," we are all looking for that particular path that will be safe and certain, and will remove the grinding fear of the uncertain.

Of course, human beings have always sought safety and certainty against the unknown. We need to have some sense of security to live our daily lives. However, the desperate quest for certainty has also clouded our thinking and blinded us to the uncertain realities of the world, and prevented us from taking clear-eyed action for growth and change. Unfortunately, this is a pretty simple process. We confuse what we "wish for" with "what is." By seeking certainty, we ignore reality, which is always uncertain.

If we confuse our wishes and desires with the reality of our lives, we will always shortchange ourselves--or worse.

But how do we reconcile our wishes and desires with the reality of our lives? The short answer: look inward. Observe yourself and the way your mind works. For example, when Donna has a fight with her husband or has an argument at work, she goes shopping. She may call it "retail therapy," but it's her way of fending off the uncertainty in her marriage or at work. She probably doesn't have any illusions that buying a new blouse will *really* solve the problems at home or on the job--it's just a temporary way of making her feel better. Eventually, if she's smart, she'll stop shopping, sit down and face her problems, and do something about them.

That's an easy example. Most of us have a lot harder time sorting out what we wish for from "what is." After fighting with our spouse, we might have fantasies of escape through divorce or having an affair. In most cases, the reality of divorce or adultery is not an escape, but just a short cut to another series of problems, often worse. The lesson is that if we confuse what we want with what is, and hop a ride on our defense mechanisms as a way of escaping uncertainty, we're probably going to end up in a worse place. Uncertainty has a way of catching up to our fantasies in terms of harsh reality.

The Culture of Certainty

It's not just our primitive minds that long for certainty. More and more, our culture plays a part in our thinking. While the quest for certainty is an age-old longing, it has taken a twist into our current "culture of certainty." Since the arrival of the scientific revolution, which really kicked into gear in the last hundred and fifty years, humanity has put much greater stock in science, in the ultimate *knowability* of everything. While most of human history has been focused on religious faith as the greatest weapon against uncertainty, the last century and a half has produced a shift to an almost equally rigid belief in science in our quest for certainty. Modern man harbors the belief (or hope) that, sooner or later, all of nature's secrets will be revealed, and reduced to empirical fact. Taken to its extreme, this implies that since everything is knowable, any phenomenon that confuses or perplexes us is merely one whose origins have yet to be discovered, or whose intricacies have yet to be observed and understood.

The power of this belief is clear. Even if we don't yet know the answer to some problem, or understand the working of some process, it's merely because we haven't yet figured out how to do so. We can take comfort in the fact that someday all that is mysterious and unknown will be explained, even if we don't possess this knowledge now. It's doing a psychological end-run around the anxiety caused by uncertainty. Ironically, science in the last half-century has almost entirely rejected this popular notion of certainty or knowability. The universe as described by scientists today is driven by randomness, chaos and uncertainty (e.g. Chaos Theory and the Heisenberg Uncertainty Principle) And this has bled over into the social sciences--from psychology to economics--which once sought to chart human behavior on some kind of ultimate graph, but now accept the randomness of human activity, whether on a personal or global scale.

Even the belief in the power of reason, or rationalism, which has been the foundation of entire edifices of knowledge--whole philosophies, branches of science, and political and social revolutions have been derived from it--has been brought into question. From Descartes to Kierkegaard, from Copernicus to Einstein, the overarching faith in empirical knowledge as the key to unlocking the secrets of the universe has been one of the dominant psychological weapons against the dread of unknowability. But now eminent philosophers and pop psychologists alike question the role of reason in human life.

While most people still cling to the idea of reason as an important, positive trait in human beings--we still talk about "common sense" as a valuable asset-- many of us are questioning the unshakeable faith in reason and science that has dominated recent human history. Science once gave us the hope that the battle against uncertainty can be won, and that we could finally triumph in our quest for certainty. (Of course, certainty was never the goal of pure science, which sought instead to *investigate* reality, and to continually challenge uncertainty, but never overcome it.) However, the failure of science to provide everything from a unified theory of physics to a cure for the common cold has left many people cynical about the ability of science or reason to address our deep fears of the unknown.

This has created a backlash against science (and reason) in the form of religious, spiritual and even political movements that embody faith over science, belief over reason, ideology over common sense. This spans the spectrum of religious belief and spirituality, from Christian fundamentalism to New Age spiritualism. For many people, a pervasive "spiritualism" that disavows reason and clings to simple superstition or iron-clad dogma is a potent defense against the vagaries of human experience. Ascribing the most distressing, inexplicable or horrifying events to "God's will" or "karma" heartens us, if only because it supports the idea that there is a guiding hand in the affairs of the universe. Whether reeling from the horror of a terror attack or the devastation of a massive *tsunami*, we fervently grasp for solace by trusting in faith. Even if we don't understand it, or fail to see the outlines of this divine plan, our belief that there is a higher purpose in what seems incomprehensible or tragically arbitrary sustains us.

Take Anne, for example. She was raised in a traditional Irish Catholic family. She has memories of going to Mass as a little girl and being awed by the mysterious incantations of the priest and the magical light that filtered through the stained glass windows. But as she grew older, Anne drifted away from the Catholic church. It seemed distant, remote and didn't seem to have much relevance to her life. However, after a bitter divorce and subsequent health crisis, Anne's life was suddenly transformed. "I became a Christian," she says simply, crediting her newly discovered faith with changing her life. Now she goes to an evangelical church and devotes her life to practicing her faith. She has a new-found certainty, at least for now.

Ironically, Anne has a lot in common with the extreme rationalists who believe whole-heartedly in science and reason. Believers in both Reason and God hold essentially the same view: we may not know the answer to our questions *now,* but there *is* an answer. And someday Reason--or God--will enlighten us. Again, the ultimate goal is to banish uncertainty. What noted Catholic author Ron Hansen calls, as a description of his faith, "A stay against confusion." For conventional believers, adherents to organized religions, much of their stated contentment comes from an unalloyed belief in their sacred texts. Radio therapist Laura Schlessinger, when discussing her life before her embrace of traditional Judaism, dismissed it as "the time when I believed that truth was subjective. I know now it isn't."

Similar sentiments were expressed on an edition of the TV show *60 Minutes* some years after 9/11, when an Iranian cleric proclaimed that the Koran must be accepted as literal truth. "Every word, every period, every comma," he intoned, or else one is an infidel. That same year, Bill O'Reilly delighted his audiences on Fox News by describing actress Jane Fonda's conversion to born-again Christianity. "She's found the Truth, with a capital T."

On the other hand, there have been many great religious figures throughout history who have rejected certainty in their faith. St. Augustine wrote in his *Confessions* about his constant crisis of faith. And even Mother Theresa, one of the most celebrated religious icons of the twentieth century, wrote in letters of her lifelong struggle with doubt about her faith.

The solace provided by religious belief--whether founded on absolute certainty or constant doubt--is not to be discounted or derided. In fact, since nothing can be known *for sure*, it's entirely possible that traditional religious believers have, indeed, the lock on the truth (with a capital "T"). But since--at least on this plane of existence--we don't as yet know whether this is so, it might be wise to reconsider utilizing pure faith in deciding, for example, on alternative medical treatment, or betting on the outcome of a football game, or even on sending troops to war.

Cultural Defense Mechanisms

In our post-modern culture of certainty, we have also developed what might be called "cultural" defense mechanisms--those unshakable political or social convictions that we see paraded all day long on cable television news, talk radio and the Internet. Men and women whose political beliefs are as rigid as steel, resistant to either compromise or even the possibility that another view has merit. Whether Michael Moore or Noam Chomsky on the left, or Bill O'Reilly and Ann Coulter on the right, these social/political pundits take no prisoners.

Why are we so fascinated by these demagogues on the extremes? Because of our yearning for certainty. Rigid political and social opinions serve as barriers against the relentless uncertainty of a changing world. After all, these are complex, befuddling times, alive with shifting social, sexual and political ideas. Long-revered institutions of church, government, and family are seemingly under assault. Gender roles have changed. Conventional wisdom about everything from crime and punishment to child-rearing to drug use is being challenged on a daily basis. Divisions between rich and poor, educated and non-educated, white and non-white, are being both deplored and exploited. And all of this delivered in a bewildering barrage of sound and images, 24/7, by a burgeoning media whose reach extends around the globe. (This is undoubtedly the Era of Opinion, and the new technological vehicles for expressing that opinion—blogs, emails, websites,

FaceBook, Huffington Post, YouTube, Twitter, and others yet to be envisioned—have only grown in support of this divisive din.)

In the face of such monumental fluidity, of rapidly-changing rules about practically everything, many people cling to rigid, doctrinaire political or social views. Hence the famous "values" debates between the political parties. No matter from which end of the political spectrum they argue, the political warriors see their fixed, often extreme, positions as valiant opposition to the dangers of the other point of view. What some might decry as "turning back the clock," others see as erecting a bulwark against a decaying, permissive, out-of-control society. What some might denounce as support for civil disorder and moral irresponsibility, others see as promoting progressive ideas against stultifying and prejudiced convention.

Not that such political jousting is new. From the formation of hierarchies of power in the various tribes of Mesopotamia, down through the ages to the latest debate between presidential rivals of nations around the world, fears of the "radical" or "dangerous" beliefs of ideological opponents has cemented political opinions into hard-line, do-or-die prejudices. Years ago, philosopher Eric Hoffer coined the phrase "true believers" to refer to people wedded to such unquestioning, unshakeable convictions.

In his recent book, *The Political Brain*, neuroscientist Drew Westen outlines his studies on the formation of political opinions deep in our brains. What Westen finds, not surprisingly, is that people form political opinions almost entirely based on emotion. Reason plays almost no part in the process. Even when people are confronted with clear evidence to contradict their opinions--for example, John Kerry's flip-flops on the war, George Bush's contradictory statements on weapons of mass destruction, or Barack Obama's backpedaling on the Afghan war--they quickly constructed a rationale to explain away the contractions. *Moreover, they emerge from this process of rationalization even more certain and rigid in their views.*

Fueled by a burning political or social agenda, these convictions--regardless of intellectual merit--are often based on the notion that to think or believe otherwise is dangerous, or even evil. In fact, what's really "dangerous" or "evil"-- what these ideologues *actually* fear-- is change, the unknown, uncertainty itself.

The United States of Uncertainty

What we're calling cultural defense mechanisms don't appear in a vacuum.

People create culture, but culture also deeply influences people, especially in a

technology-driven mass culture. In the Middle Ages, people feared most the

ravages of the plague and the desolation of famine, both of which arrived with

enough unpredictable regularity as to make the anxiety of daily living its only

predictable aspect. When you add in the almost constant threat of invasion and

conquest, you have a real appreciation of the poet's description of such a life as

"nasty, brutish and short."

Today, however, our fears are more generalized, but no less real. Modern

America clearly qualifies as the United States of Uncertainty. Our lives are filled

with uncertainty, fueled by the complexity of our social systems and our fast-

paced, technology-driven life. The demands of work and marriage, the pressures

of money, the responsibilities of modern parenthood, not to mention the changing

roles of men and women, can lead to profound feelings of inadequacy,

incomprehension and alienation. While the roots of this uncertainty may be more

abstract than the hungry tiger lurking outside our cave, they are nonetheless very

real. Let's look at some very real sources of that uncertainty in our modern world.

We live in a global economy that is fraught with uncertainty. With

instantaneous global communications, multinational markets and fierce competition, globalization has deepened our sense of uncertainty a thousandfold. Depending on how you look at it, it's either a tremendous opportunity or a Darwinian race for economic survival. However, the fact is that, whether you're an office worker in Cleveland or an entrepreneur in Houston (or a factory worker in China or Mexico), globalization means uncertainty. From the outsourcing of jobs to dynamic emerging markets, globalization is rapidly changing our workplace, our finances and our lives. And that rapid change has brought more uncertainty than ever.

Technology, which is developing at an unprecedented rate, has also added greatly to the uncertainty of our lives. From workers who have been displaced by sophisticated machines and computers to traditional rituals like the family dinner conversation, which has been replaced by a confusing mix of texting, social media and TV viewing, we have all experienced the unsettling impact of technology. While technology has offered us many opportunities, it has also created a future that is less certain than ever.

How about the American Dream itself? In decades past, job security was guaranteed for the "company man." But today, with fierce global competition and rapid technological change, not to mention the onset of the Great Recession, most workers expect not only to change companies, but also to change careers several times during their working lives. That is if they are lucky enough to get and keep a job. A job loss by either husband or wife, a medical crisis, a hike in health premiums or a stock market setback can mean hardship or even disaster. And as work itself has become more uncertain, the dynamics of the workplace have become both more fraught and more flexible. Anyone who is looking for certainty in pay, promotion or profit will surely be disappointed.

Another heavy dose of uncertainty came on September 11, 2001. With the terrorist attacks on the United States, followed by the wars in Iraq and Afghanistan, our world became a more dangerous and frightening place. America responded to those attacks by declaring a "global war on terrorism," which has achieved decidedly mixed results. The national budget for homeland security has doubled since 9/11 – nearly $200 billion since the attacks. But are we any safer? The chances of dying in a terrorist attack are infinitesimally small compared to dying in a car accident, for example. However, we still respond with almost primal fear at the prospect of future attacks. Accepting uncertainty in the face of terrorist threats doesn't mean passively giving up on public safety. But it does mean making a realistic assessment of the risk.

At the same time, we're more aware than ever of our powerlessness over global forces. Uprisings in the Middle East, tribal wars in northern Africa. Jihads and taped messages from extremists on Al Jazeera. There's a simmering frustration with these new realities and a nostalgia for earlier, simpler times –

which has led to the kind of polarization that casts all conflicts in terms of good and evil, right and wrong, left and right. As a result, our society has become more splintered and divisive. Moreover, we ignore the complex realities underlying our greatest problems, from globalization to environmental change and war.

For example: Our health has always been a concern for human beings, but the advent of modern medical science has succeeded in removing some of the uncertainty around our health. Yet illness, and ultimately death, are inevitable. However, we understandably fear this basic truth, and in some ways, actually deny it. Of course, we can take prudent measures to prevent illness, but the notion of eliminating all risks to health and safety is not only absurd, it can be emotionally damaging.

Not that we're not trying. Spending on health care is nearly $2 trillion annually, with another $100 billion spent on medical research. While all these efforts promise healthier, longer lives, they also serve to maintain the anxiety about death which pervades the culture. By stressing quantity of life at the expense of quality, there's the danger of creating an ever-upward-spiraling expectation of medical miracles, without the concurrent examination of what actually gives life meaning, regardless of its length. Paradoxically, some of the newest advances in medicine and well-being incorporate aspects of the very uncertainty we're trying to dispel: i.e., the mental and physical benefits of mind-body work like yoga, meditation and other systems come about not by willing them, but rather by a surrender of control, a yielding to the inevitable.

We are also facing more uncertainty in our personal relationships than ever before. With shifting gender roles, parenting styles and social mores--not to mention the economic pressures on everyone--it is harder to navigate the uncertain landscape of relationships. Life is constant change, and this is especially true of relationships. If we're paralyzed by the fear of any change, in ourselves and those we love, we will not be able to take risks in our relationships. However, if we accept at least *some* uncertainty in even our most important relationships, we will be able to take greater risks and reap greater rewards.

After almost thirty years of research, marriage expert John Gottman concluded that *emotional flexibility and acceptance of risk* are the most important components to maintaining trust and intimacy within a couple. In fact, the latest statistics from family therapy surveys and clinical studies show that the entire family system requires this level of fluidity and risk acceptance. Since nothing is ever certain, even those people who are closest to us will inevitably change--and along with them, the relationship. Living with the risk, uncertainty and changing dynamics of a relationship, though sometimes difficult, is the key to keeping it vital and healthy.

Perhaps no other area has been as disrupted by the uncertainty of our times as religion. Where religion once was a bedrock of certainty in a world full of doubt, religious institutions are now wracked with upheaval and uncertainty. It's true that religion itself is a paradox. It's built upon the absolute certainty of faith, yet at the same time extols the mystery at the heart of creation. Too often in human history, usually for purely political or cultural reasons, the doubt that is essential to faith is replaced by a dogmatic, even destructive certainty. And yet, all people are searching for answers in uncertain times, and most religions are struggling to provide some answers--or at least a plausible narrative--to the mystery of God and faith.

A Few Words on Behalf of Fear...

Our society has a pretty jaundiced view of fear. "Fear is not an option" is the current credo. Fear is considered a sign of weakness or a character flaw. And for most people, when facing a threat, better confidence than fear. Hell, better *arrogance* than fear--even if rooted in ignorance and folly.

When Franklin D. Roosevelt famously said that "we have nothing to fear but fear itself," he wasn't saying that we should be afraid of fear. Quite the opposite. *Fear is a natural response to dangers, real or imagined.* What FDR meant is that the danger can be overcome, and therefore we should not succumb blindly to our fears. In fact, fear has gotten a bad rap. We are forever trying to banish our fears, to summon our courage and dismiss all doubt. But by doing so, we fail to appreciate the positive role that fear plays in our emotional, biological, and creative well-being--thus ignoring its value as a tool for growth and change.

So how are we coping with our fear here in the United States of Uncertainty? The answer is: not that well. For the most part, our cultural defense mechanisms--the coping strategies we devise, consciously or unconsciously, to help contain our anxiety about the real and imagined dangers of life--*themselves* breed uncertainty and fear. Barbara Ehrenreich's seminal *Fear of Falling*, and similar books, correctly identify both the internal and external pressures on the middle class. If, as these works maintain, most people feel daily the dread of financial ruin in the face of an uncertain economy, it goes a long way toward explaining our collective drive toward achievement and success. Moreover, our awareness that others are striving for the same level of achievement and monetary security fuels the fierce sense of competition that underlies much of our social, professional and political interactions.

As a society, it seems clear that we're all afraid of "falling"--that is, losing our tentative grip on personal, financial and emotional security--especially in these tough economic times. Though we in the West are frequently denounced for being rampant consumers, what we're often buying with our new and fully-loaded cars, our closet full of trendy clothes, our growing inventory of the latest technological devices, our iPods and iPhones, our yoga and Pilates classes, our graduate degrees and wine-tasting workshops and weekly book clubs, our eco-friendly wilderness vacations--the whole overstuffed cornucopia of *things* that author Tom Wolfe calls "status details"--what we're often really buying is the illusion of continuing safety and social stability. In other words, as consumers, what we ourselves are actually consumed with is banishing uncertainty. Eliminating doubt. Maintaining the status quo by constantly increasing the quality and quantity of those material things required to do so. A high-achiever on Wall Street, on deciding to drop out of the rat race, famously declared, "I'm tired of doing things I don't want to do, to buy things I don't want, to impress people I don't like."

Unfortunately, most of us fall into this trap of keeping up with the Jones. Why? To banish the specter of uncertainty. A writer on the former TV sitcom *The Cosby Show* tells the story of his boss, Bill Cosby, returning one Monday morning to the set after an exhausting weekend flying around the country doing comedy routines at big venues. "Why do you do it, Bill?" the writer asked. "You've got a hit show, lots of money in the bank, and a big career." Cosby shrugged, then his shoulders slumped. "The housing projects, man," he said. "I don't want to ever go back there." Cosby, like all of us, was haunted by his own personal fear and uncertainty, implausible as it may seem for one of the most successful and intelligent entertainers of our era.

Striving to better oneself and one's circumstances is a good thing, of course. At the societal level, such diligence leads to creativity and innovation, much of which translates into pragmatic, practical improvements and advances that truly benefit the whole. But it's important to remember that many of us cling to the fantasy of wealth and achievement as self-protective ends in themselves. After all, more people buy lottery tickets now than at any time in history. The dream of the big score--a bounty of riches so huge that all worries, financial and otherwise, crumble beneath it--is one of the prime fantasies wielded against the insecurity of the present and the uncertainty of the future. However, most lottery winners, when questioned five years after their windfall, state categorically that they wished

they'd never won.

Rejecting Certainty

In a famous scene from the classic movie *The Graduate,* a young Dustin Hoffman gets some unsolicited advice from a friend of his parents. "Go into plastics, son. That's the future." Hoffman takes the advice with a heavy dose of skepticism, as he should. How many well-meaning people have heard this kind of tried-and-true (and usually completely wrong) wisdom?

Bill Gates' father thought he was crazy to drop out of Harvard to start a little company called Microsoft. "Why would anybody ever want a 'personal' computer?" asked Bill Gates, Sr. When a Texas housewife enlisted friends to sell cosmetics to other women in their homes, people were convinced it would never fly. Now Mary Kay Cosmetics is a textbook case study at Harvard Business School.

And it's not just in the business world that conventional wisdom is almost always wrong. Whether in relationships, parenting, career choices, consumer decisions and a host of other human interactions, we search for certainty at our peril.

Take Phil and Beth, for example. Their eight-year-old son Todd had been having problems in school, and one of his teachers suggested they have him tested for Attention Deficit Hyperactivity Disorder. After he tested positive, a specialist recommended medication to help Todd in school with his academic and social problems.

This precipitated a huge argument between Phil, who rejected the idea of medication out of hand, and Beth, who felt that medication might help their son. Pretty soon, their friends got involved, staking out both sides of the argument. Some were aghast that they would "dope" their child, others said it was worth a try. Phil and Beth devoured books on the subject and listened to the raging debate on the talk shows.   In the end, they decided to give the medication a try. The results were mixed. Todd's academic performance improved markedly, but he became more withdrawn. After a few months, they reduced the dosage. His grades went down, but he became more outgoing. Finally, after a year and a half, Todd went off the medication completely. Years later, he graduated from high school with decent--not great--grades and is attending a good college.

In retrospect, both Todd and his parents believe they made the right decision. Rather than taking a rigid position "for or against" medication, they embraced the uncertainty of their predicament. They gave it a try. The results were mixed, but were probably right for them. Most importantly, it gave Todd a realistic perspective on his ADHD. Rather than being hamstrung between a rigid, all-or-nothing approach to treatment, he acknowledged the complexity of the challenge and, along with his parents, adopted a flexible, realistic strategy.

Let's face it: embracing uncertainty is more difficult for some people than others. In large measure, how we defend against uncertainty depends on both our nature and our nurture. Remember, our defense mechanisms are neither good nor bad: they simply *are*, as a conscious or unconscious bulwark against uncertainty. And how they're deployed by an individual has so much to do with that person's genetic makeup and environmental experience, from childhood onwards, that any attempt to parse out whether certain defenses are learned or inherent is futile.

Of course, someone raised in a family where feelings were suppressed, or communication about one's troubles was considered unseemly or even dangerous, is likely to carry into adulthood a persona heavily invested in decorum, the primacy of logic in discussion, and the avoidance of confrontation. In addition, he or she would be deeply suspicious of, or even doubtful about, the veracity of strongly-expressed emotions. People sharing such feelings would be characterized as too sensitive, or perhaps needy and unstable. Conversely, someone raised in a volatile, highly verbal family might believe that *only* extroverted, expressive people are genuine and engaged, and thus entertains suspicions about the enthusiasm, interest and warm-heartedness of timid or reticent people.

What each person must grasp is that neither one is seeing the truth, but rather seeing each other, and the world at large, through the prism of their own individual subjective experiences. And, according to leading psychoanalytic theorist Robert

Stolorow, the way these experiences are "organized"--in other words, what *meaning* we give to our experiences--forms our impression and understanding of how the world "works." Simply put, human beings are meaning-makers. We give things--feelings, experiences, thoughts, expectations--specific meanings. And it's to confirm or deny these meanings that we develop conscious and unconscious defense mechanisms.

Take Raymond, for example. Growing up in a family where feelings of doubt or fear were ridiculed or dismissed gave him the message that he should never show fear, or even admit doubt to himself. Now, as an adult, Raymond is stuck in a dead-end job, but he's afraid to change careers because of economic uncertainty. This might, in fact, be a pretty sensible decision. But Raymond's internal voices from his childhood label his fears of changing jobs with a harsh, specific meaning--namely, that he's a wimp, a coward, unadventurous. To quell this internal tension, and to keep shame at bay, he adopted a stance of stoic acceptance.

Now Raymond even takes pride in his stoicism. He's developed a creed for himself: "I've made my bed, now I have to lie in it." "People who go from job to job are unsure of themselves and their goals." "A bird in the hand is worth two in the bush." Raymond views his job stability and commitment as the marks of true maturity. Whether conscious or not, Raymond now operates out of a defense mechanism so pervasive and consistent that for him--and everyone who knows him--it's just his "personality." And yet he's still unhappy.

None of us are immune to this process. Our experiences give birth to a set of meanings we embrace, a sort of mythology about how the world works, and we develop conscious and unconscious defense mechanisms tailored to meet its demands. The problem is, as we've discussed, *there is no one way the world works*--and therefore no one way to deal with it. If nothing else, our fight-or-flight response is a physiological confirmation of this sober truth, no matter what defense mechanisms we construct.

Which brings us back to our terrified caveman, facing a hungry saber-tooth tiger: one of the more erudite and reflective cavemen in his tribe, let's say that he's adopted vegetarianism as a life philosophy, both for its "empathy-for-all-living-things" that he's proud to assert and as a result of his revulsion at the sight of slain animals. In our view, his vegetarianism is both a noble position and a probably unconscious defense mechanism. Regardless, as he stands alone in the wild, frozen to the spot by the competing urges of the fight-or-flight response, one thing seems clear: his being a vegetarian is unlikely to have much effect on the charging saber-tooth. As a defense mechanism, at least in this particular instance, it's going to fall woefully short.

Which is why it's important that we try to deconstruct our defense mechanisms. Not to dismantle them--this is both unwise and frequently impossible--but to make sure we understand them. Otherwise, these defense systems, like walls protecting us from the uncertain and unknowable, can end up making us prisoners of our fears. Walled in by our own walls.

Remember, defense mechanisms are inevitable and necessary. Don't leave home without them. But, at the same time, *lifelong defenses that go unrecognized and unexamined actually prevent us from confronting those aspects of ourselves we're trying to defend against, and thus prevent us from growing and changing.*

Understanding our own defenses is crucial if we're to live more authentically in the world. If we're to accept, tolerate and ultimately embrace the uncertainty of life--and thus unleash the potential for creativity, positive change and personal growth this can bring--we need first to recognize and explore our unique defenses. We must ask ourselves: Do our political beliefs limit our open-mindedness to different ideas? Does the faith we have in reason blind us to the solace and wisdom to be found in spiritual pursuits? Does our adherence to religious dogma require that we discount the moral probity of those who don't believe? Does our strict observance of conventional technique prevent us from exploring new ways of doing things? Is our death-grip on what we feel is the "known" preventing us from reaching, if only with a single finger, for the unknown?

The idea that we need to acknowledge and examine the origins and protective value of our defense mechanisms is easy to grasp. But not easy to do. If you do it right, it can take a lifetime. But we believe the potential rewards are worth it.

Moreover, it's only by doing so that we can finally understand that our defenses – the walls erected around us against uncertainty – are of our own making, and thus have the potential to not only protect us, but to imprison us as well.

Freeing ourselves from that prison takes courage, as well as a willingness to look within. Yet ultimately each of us can decide to take that risk, to make that effort, to reach for our untapped personal potential. As, funnily enough, we're reminded by the lyrics of an old song by The Eagles:

"So often times it happens, that we live our lives in chains--

And we never even know we have the key…"

Embracing Uncertainty

We've all experienced times of great uncertainty. A health crisis. A rocky marriage. A stressful job. And these crises can tap into our deepest fears of the uncertain, the unknowable, the unforeseen.

How do we respond? Because uncertainty is so painful, we too often seek the quickest resolution of that pain. We flee from the unhappy marriage. Quit the job. Try to escape through denial or addiction. Or, hungering for simple solutions, we bury our heads in the sands of fixed and rigid certainty. We cling to dogma, science, prejudice. Put our trust in gurus, unyielding political beliefs or divisive ideologies.

But there is another way.

Embracing uncertainty—rather than seeking to banish or ignore it---is in fact the only way to utilize its power. To mine its vast potential as a source of creativity, authenticity, and personal and professional growth. Fear and uncertainty are, in fact, the wellsprings of positive change. Rather than trying to banish fear and doubt, or struggle against the reality of uncertainty, we should view uncertainty--and our own fears--as a part of the normal state of nature, and of human life and society.

Only by embracing the power of uncertainty can we open doors to a world of greater creativity, accomplishment and fulfillment, both as individuals and as a society.

Embracing uncertainty is *not* about ridding our lives of all certainty, or becoming crippled by doubt. Instead, it's about finding a balance in our lives between "what is" and what we wish for. It's about navigating the healthy landscape between dreams and reality, conviction and pragmatism, fear and courage, both as individuals and as a society.

In our struggle against the uncertainty of modern life--whether in terms of increasing global instability and decreasing economic confidence, dizzying changes in our social and cultural institutions, or upheavals in our personal relationships--we often succumb to prejudice and "conventional wisdom." In our quest for certainty, we give in to divisive, black-or-white thinking that seeks to address the most complex questions with iron-clad religious doctrines, simplistic political slogans, or an "us versus them" mentality.

From breakthroughs in physics, to new paradigms revolutionizing business, psychology and politics, uncertainty is best viewed as a dynamic natural state.

From Weapons of Mass Destruction in Iraq ("It's a slam dunk!") to seeking "the Twelve Rules of Happiness," we yearn for certainty. After all, it's a short trip from "I believe" to "I know what's right"--and an even shorter one to "You're either with us or against us." And this is true in everything from personal relationships to the world of business.

Case in point: When Southwest Airlines was the new kid on the block, it aimed to turn its airplanes around on the tarmac in less than forty-five minutes. Airline industry veterans scoffed at the idea. "Impossible," they said, with the certainty of conventional wisdom and experience. But Southwest took a leap into uncertainty, tossed out the rules and looked at the real challenges. Turnaround time at Southwest is now as little as fifteen minutes.

Uncertainty--and along with it, fear and doubt--is a natural part of the human condition and our world. We now understand that the complex behavior of human beings--whether as individuals or as members of society--is often analogous to the tenets of uncertainty theory in physics. In politics and international affairs, in economics and finance, in psychology and social theory--even in religion, the arts and health care--the dynamic reality of uncertainty has overshadowed the rigid and fixed systems of the past.

The greatest weapon against fear is knowledge. We belive that embracing the reality of uncertainty is crucial to growth and success. The fact is, people who are "doers"--those who create, innovate, and succeed--live daily with uncertainty. When Albert Einstein was asked once how he worked, he replied, "I grope."

Each of us has the power--and the tools--to embrace uncertainty.

The first step on this path is to understand and accept how we, as individuals and as a culture, are gripped by a powerful yearning for certainty. In our quest for this elusive certainty, we can become too fixed in our opinions and too certain in our path. We're unwilling to take risks, or challenge our own long-held views

Moreover, we tend to shut out others when their behavior or beliefs clash with our own. We miss opportunities for growth or enrichment because they don't fit into our customary view of "how things are done." And we stifle creativity, and thus potential personal and professional growth, by clinging to the beliefs and prejudices of the past.

So what are the tools we can use to embrace uncertainty? Here are a few:

Toss out the rules: The tried and true is usually dead wrong.

Put fear and doubt to work for you: Fear and doubt are our greatest tools for change. Learn to recognize the power of uncertainty.

Reject certainty: People who tell you that they are absolutely certain about something-- whether they're friends, lovers or political leaders--are not only misguided, but often dangerous, both personally and professionally.

Fear-- feel it, face it, use it: "We have nothing to fear but fear itself," goes the famous quote from FDR. He wasn't saying we should shrink from our fears. Quite the opposite. What he was saying was that danger and uncertainty can be overcome, and therefore we should not react blindly and impulsively to our fears. If we can embrace our fears--and understand the self-defeating meanings we give to them--we will open ourselves to a universe of change. If we shut them out and deny them, we are shutting the door on growth and change.

The era of certainty may be over--and it should be. As Antonio Machado wrote, "Traveler, there is no path. Paths are made by walking."

But for those who embrace uncertainty, and begin to walk their own path, the possibilities that wait around the next, unseen corner represent the beginning of a new, equally unimaginable era.

ABOUT THE AUTHORS

Hoyt Hilsman

Hoyt is an award-winning writer and critic, and a former candidate for Congress in California. He has written screenplays for the major studios and networks, and hundreds of articles for national newspapers and magazines, including *The New York Times, The Los Angeles Times, Hemispheres, Emmy* and *The National Law Journal.* He is a regular contributor to *The Huffington Post,* is a former critic for *Variety,* and is a recipient of the Apex Award for Journalism. His novel *19 Angels,* a political thriller, was published in the fall of 2010.

Hoyt grew up in Washington, DC, where his father was an advisor to President Kennedy and head of Intelligence for the State Department. He has been active in politics ever since, working with various national figures, including Bill Clinton, and as an advisor to several Congressional campaigns. He has been a director at the Hope Street Group, a policy think tank, and a member of the Pacific Council on International Policy. He has also been a consultant to a number of corporations, non-profits and governmental organizations, including The Kennedy Space Center and Idealab!

For more info, please visit www.hoythilsman.com

Dennis Palumbo

Formerly a Hollywood screenwriter (*My Favorite Year; Welcome Back, Kotter,* etc.), Dennis is now a licensed psychotherapist and author of *Writing From the Inside Out* (John Wiley). His work helping writers has been profiled in *The New York Times, The Los Angeles Times, GQ* and other publications, as well as on CNN, NPR and PBS. He also blogs regularly for *The Huffington Post.*
His mystery fiction has appeared in *Ellery Queen's Mystery Magazine, The Strand, Written By* and elsewhere, and is collected in *From Crime to Crime* (Tallfellow Press). His crime novel, *Mirror Image* (Poisoned Pen Press), is the first in a new series featuring psychologist Daniel Rinaldi, a trauma expert who consults with the Pittsburgh Police. The sequel, *Fever Dream,* was published in 2011.

For more info, please visit www.dennispalumbo.com